THE SCULPTURE OF
JOHN B. FLANNAGAN

Triumph of the Egg I. Granite, 1937. The Museum of Modern Art.

THE SCULPTURE OF JOHN B. FLANNAGAN

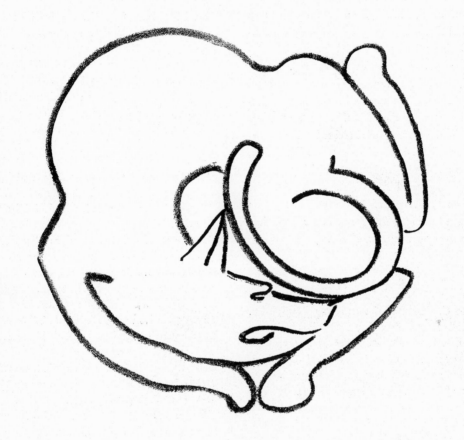

EDITED BY DOROTHY C. MILLER
INTRODUCTION BY CARL ZIGROSSER
AND A STATEMENT BY THE ARTIST

THE MUSEUM OF MODERN ART · NEW YORK

ACKNOWLEDGMENTS

The President and Trustees of the Museum of Modern Art and the Director of the Exhibition, Dorothy C. Miller, wish to thank those who have lent works of art from their collections to the exhibition. Invaluable assistance has been given by Mr. Carl Zigrosser, who has generously contributed the introduction to the catalog and has supplied important information about the sculpture. Mrs. John B. Flannagan, Miss Laura Canadé and Mr. Curt Valentin have also been of great assistance in assembling the exhibition and the catalog. In addition, the Museum is indebted to the following: Edward W. Forbes, Mrs. Juliana R. Force, Bartlett H. Hayes, Jr., Horace H. F. Jayne, Miss Agnes Rindge, and Dr. W. R. Valentiner. The American Federation of Arts has permitted the use in the catalog of *The Image in the Rock*, first published in the *Magazine of Art*.

TRUSTEES OF THE MUSEUM

HONORARY TRUSTEES

STAFF OF THE MUSEUM

CONTENTS

Illustration on cover and title page: Crayon
study for granite *Dog,* 1932-33 (No. 53)

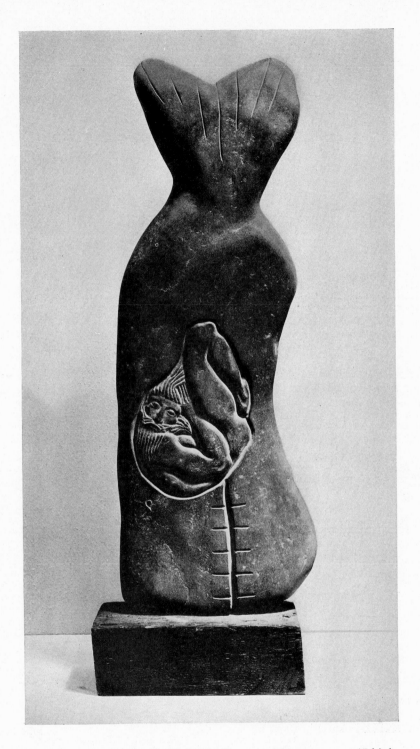

Jonah and the Whale: Rebirth Motif. 1937. Bluestone, 30½″ high.
Lent by the Weyhe Gallery.

6

THE IMAGE IN THE ROCK

OFTEN THERE IS an occult attraction in the very shape of a rock as sheer abstract form. It fascinates with a queer atavistic nostalgia, as either a remote memory or a stirring impulse from the depth of the unconscious.

That's the simple sculptural intention. As design, the eventual carving involuntarily evolves from the eternal nature of the stone itself, an abstract linear and cubical fantasy out of the fluctuating sequence of consciousness, expressing a vague general memory of many creatures, of human and animal life in its various forms.

It partakes of the deep pantheistic urge of kinship with all living things and fundamental unity of all life, a unity so complete it can see a figure of dignity even in the form of a goat. Many of the humbler life forms are often more useful as design than the narcissistic human figure, because, humanly, we project ourselves into all art works using the human figure, identifying ourselves with the beauty, grace, or strength of the image as intense wish fulfillment; and any variant, even when necessitated by design, shocks as maimed, and produces some psychological pain. With an animal form, on the contrary, any liberty taken with the familiar forms is felt as amusing—strange cruelty.

To that instrument of the subconscious, the hand of a sculptor, there exists an image within every rock. The creative act of realization merely frees it.

The stone cutter, worker of metal, painter, those who think and feel by hand, are timeless, haunted by all the old dreams. The artist remembers, or else is fated by cosmic destiny to serve as the instrument for realizing in visible form the profound subterranean urges of the human spirit in the whole dynamic life process—birth, growth, decay, death.

The stone carving of an alligator called *Dragon Motif* was simply chiseled with primary interest in the abstract circular design. Yet in so doing fascinated by something of the wonder and terror that must have made the fearsome monster fantasy—an old dream. Vitalized by that perfect design pattern, the circle, fitting symbol of eternity, the movement is both peripheral and centrifugal. Restless, it moves ever onward, finally to turn back into itself, an endless movement.

With such abstract purpose, instead of classic poise, there is more of the dynamic tension that is movement, even accentuated by devices that are restless such as a deliberate lack of obvious balance in design and the use of repetition to heighten the occult activity with velocity, as in the psyche of our time—speed without pauses or accents.

Even in our time, however, we yet know the great longing and hope of the ever recurrent and still surviving dream, the wishful rebirth fantasy, *Jonah and the Whale—Rebirth Motif*. It's eerie to learn that the fish is the very ancient symbol of the female principle.

In the austere elimination of the accidental for ordered simplification, there is a quality of the abstract and lifeless, but lifeless only contra spurious lifelikeness. Instead of which a purely sculptural attempt by the most simple unambiguous demonstration of tactile relations, the greatest possible preservation of cubic compactness, carved to exclude all chance evasive spatial aspects to approximate the abstract cubical elemental forms and even to preserve the identity of the original rock so that it hardly seems carved, rather to have endured so always—inevitable.

The artistic representation of the organic and living now takes on an abstract lifeless order and becomes, instead of the likeness of what is conditioned, the symbol of what is unconditioned and invariable, as though seeking the timeless, changeless finality of death. Sculpture like this is as inevitable.

All as part of the profound social purpose of art—communication. We communicate something of the record of the human spirit.

JOHN B. FLANNAGAN
June, 1941

JOHN B. FLANNAGAN

There is a theory about the origin of art that is exemplified by the oyster that creates the pearl. Art—in this case the pearl—comes about through irritation and pain and suffering. If the theory has any plausibility, it is borne out in the life of John B. Flannagan.

Flannagan had a tragic life. This is not the occasion to analyze his psyche or to enumerate the handicaps and malign forces which frustrated his personal life from childhood on. The story has unfolded to its tragic dénouement, and may some day be told—portrayed in the mood and with the complex overtones of a Dostoyevsky character. He was a distinguished artist and it is as an artist that I shall speak of him. His art was not tragic: it was pure and self-contained, profound yet simple.

He once set forth his credo in a letter*:"My aim is to produce sculpture as direct and swift in feeling as drawing—sculpture with such ease, freedom, and simplicity that it hardly seems carved but rather to have endured so always. This accounts for my preference for field stone: its very rudeness seems to me more in harmony with simple direct statement. There are often necessary compromises, but the shape of the stone does not determine the design; more often the design dictates the choice of the stone. I would like my sculpture to appear as rocks, left quite untouched and natural, and, as you have said, inevitable. Such qualities of humor or the grotesque or whatever may be found therein are for the most part accidental and

*A volume of the letters of John B. Flannagan, with an introduction by W. R. Valentiner, is now in preparation.

subordinate to a conception purely sculptural."

In the above he hints at one of the two leading themes he once elaborated to me as being dominant in his attitude—a passion for anonymity. The work itself, and not the artist, was important; the ultimate end and not the instrument. The work was enduring and timeless, the artist merely human and temporal. Why should there be this modern cult of the so-called creator? Do we know who *created* Egyptian or Assyrian sculpture, who carved the Cathedral of Chartres? "In the Middle Ages the unknown man carved the numberless statues of Romanesque and Gothic cathedrals, and covered chapel and refectory walls with unsigned frescoes. But with the approach to modern times, when the stupid craze for signatures came in, the unknown man ceased his activity and was content to rest. An immense throng of vain fellows, of men who had a name or sought to make a name, began to paint, invent, carve, write. They had less genius than the unknown man and they also had less modesty; they proclaimed to all the winds that they, and none but they, had done these things. They worked not only for their own joy or for others' benefit, but that the world might know that they, and none but they, had done the work." Very few of Flannagan's sculptures are signed, except insofar as they are signed all over. He was medieval in his disinterested and truly mystical passion for humility and anonymity. St. Francis of Assisi was one of his great heroes. He would have felt at home in the Middle Ages, and he might

9

perhaps have led a happier life in the age of universal faith. He would have liked nothing better than to have had his work merge into the great anonymous plastic tradition of Egypt or medieval Europe, but it seems more than likely that his desire for anonymity will not be granted him.

The other theme he stressed was what he called the philosophy of pity. This philosophy had reverberations in his personal life, but in his art it was related to his sympathy for all living things, particularly the humbler animals (St. Francis again), his *feeling into* whatever subject he approached: "The intense feeling of identification," as he put it, "with which I take up each stone to work upon it." He wrote in his notes: "Embrace all living forms, each for its plastic adjustment to a theme—living for warmth. No narcissistic worship of humanity—contra, the stately dignity of the Mountain Goat, the ironic pensiveness of the apparently thoughtful Monkey, and (in his greater moments) the timeless yet rebellious patience of the Ass." There is an all too human logic in this attitude which he subtly analyzed in *The Image in the Rock* (see page 7).

His work was executed with unbelievable intensity. When the fury of creation descended on him, he worked quite literally night and day without pause. "Creation is revelation," he said. The physical labor of direct carving, intense and exhausting though it be, was merely the stripping away of extraneous material, revealing the image which he had projected in the rock. There was no floundering around in conception or execution. His esthetic intuitions were immediate and absolute, and his hand with practised cunning made them concrete. But there were fallow periods. He who had such spiritual

need for certainty fell prey to devastating uncertainty and doubt. He would lose faith in himself, his past work and his future inspiration. Then he would strive to forget, to escape by any means at hand this awful inchoate dread, the dark night of the soul. In this vein he once wrote me: "This past summer has been one of constant strain—a tension that has drawn me as taut as a violin string. Believe me I am trying, but I am not always successful. Always I am seeing with the vividness of a hallucination the wraithlike figure of a child that seems irrevocably lost; and the only way I see to dissipate my own feeling of being equally lost myself, is to give you a show expressing everything I have to say just now. After that I'm safe." "All artists," he said on another occasion, "are close to madness; it is their art that keeps them sane." In another mood, however, he could write serenely: "I feel like a different person. It was a case of going stale before I left, but now I find there is still something eager left in me—so much so, that I don't even feel the need of a drink any more, but feel more intensely just one steady abiding purpose such as it is—to make images out of rock. There is here a certain quiet I have sought for a long time. There is peace in the unhurried and simple existence of life here, so that I, in relishing it, feel out of place in the highly mechanized drift of our time, and have found where I belong."

Paradoxically enough, Flannagan was both apart from and of his time. He stood apart from it in that he was essentially a mystic, one who aligned himself with spirit rather than mechanism. He was modern by reason of his intelligent grasp of the problems of the artist today. What he admired about the Middle Ages was the functional relation, the

10

give and take, between the artist and society, and between art and architecture. Today, he felt, both these relations were to a large extent ignored. He saw the necessity of re-establishing these values. In his application for a Guggenheim Fellowship in 1931 he cited as one of his chief aims a study of the "co-ordination of sculpture and architecture as expressed notably in 13th century Gothic, the ultimate purpose being the simplification of sculptural design and structure so as to be effective in the severe architectural scheme prevailing now." And in a note recently written: "Just as all really effective art has been an expression of the psyche of its time, so the simplification prevalent in the best contemporary art is quite in step with the severity of our architecture. It would seem also that the very austerity of that architectural style necessarily demands discreet sculptural relief."

Flannagan was always interested in the application of sculpture to building, but he never really had a chance to put his ideas into practice. The nearest he came to it was perhaps the *Design for a Skyscraper Court*, the *Mother and Child*, now in the Fogg Museum (see page 27). He made the design for Rockefeller Center, but it never came officially before the authorities. Nevertheless, he decided to execute it on a large scale. He made an illuminating analysis of the problems involved in a monumental sculpture to be placed in a court surrounded by high buildings. A statue in the round, he reasoned, must be designed to compose well from every angle, in this case not only when seen from the ground but also from above, from the many windows of the surrounding skyscrapers. This complicated set of conditions he solved triumphantly in what is, in my

opinion, one of the most important works of modern sculpture in America.

He was modern, too, in his consistent preoccupation with abstraction. It was always fundamental in his design, but he fused and modified it with other factors. "Pure abstraction is dead," he said. "Make it come alive by the use of living form. Warm the cold geometry of abstraction with a naturalism in which the superficial and accidental have been eliminated by their union with pure form. A withdrawing from the too close view of things in order to see them in their atmospheric content. Use abstraction to achieve a finality, but, in humanizing it with immediacy, retain it always in a state of becoming, rather than being. A thing should never be finished—should rather always be in a state of *becoming* (no end: an evasion or overcoming of time), completed each according to his own psyche by whoever has eyes to see. Use the apparently accidental to avoid formal hardness, and the spontaneous to avoid emotional hardness. A fine composition has the calm ordered elation of a mathematical solution, instead of mock-heroics or maudlin-nostalgic-associational emotionalism." It is obvious that with such a conception of the basis of art, consistently avoiding any formula or superficial mannerism, Flannagan could only be a lone creator and never the founder of a school. Yet, as has happened with John Marin, imitators have managed to discover a bag of surface tricks without ever penetrating to the animating spirit within. Thus Flannagan has not been without influence as a master of direct carving in America today.

He was no escapist. Long ago he spoke of "disciplining myself to think and see and feel so naturally as to escape the precious or the

11

esoteric. My aim is the achievement of a sculpture that should fulfill a definite function in the social consciousness of many instead of a limited few." He accepted the realities of today. Escapism he associated with the romantic attitude and he abhorred it. "Science honest—romance evasion and dishonest. Honesty liberates—cutting away romance and sentiment—deals with hard realities instead of dead moralities and high sentimental purities." In a letter to Curt Valentin enclosing the manuscript of *The Image in the Rock* he wrote: "Here is my credo —some week-end reading—I hope it reads well—it has clarity for those who make the effort toward intelligence. For the others, the Escapists, have their comic strip and Walt Disney. This statement has nothing of that flight from reality, the romantic, and neither have I."

His work was always keyed to the sculptural needs of today: monumental statues when he had the opportunity (the *Design for a Skyscraper Court* and the *Gold Miner* in Fairmount Park, Philadelphia, demonstrate with what success he solved the problems of plastic monumentality); sculpture for gardens, and small pieces designed for the home. His work has a direct human appeal without ever departing from the plastic conventions. Sculpture is an austere art, one that requires mature planning and sustained effort in its execution. Therefore he chose themes of a universal or symbolic nature—woman, man, child, animal. The design, the sculptural form, was, as we have seen, the keystone of his conception, but he vitalized it with living subject matter. Over and above the tactile organization of his lines, planes, and masses there seems to brood the mystery and glamor of a living thing. Thus he created character

and psychological values as well as esthetic forms.

Flannagan had an unusually developed plastic sense, a perception of three-dimensional form. Possibly only a sculptor can appreciate the daring and rightness of his simplification of planes, the solidity of his masses, and the inner logic of his forms. He was a great technician. His knowledge of the idiosyncracies of wood and stone and metal and the mechanics of the sculptor's craft was unsurpassed. But he had gone far beyond mere technique, which he called "hardness— the display of obvious skill and an overdone imitation of the surface aspects of reality." He believed in understatement, disdaining ostentatious facility. He once wrote: "It takes an artist to be a really good craftsman; all that these shop-trained guys know are things one *can't do;* but we artists say *can do* with imagination." "Thinking with his hands," as he used to call it, he could be more receptive to psychological overtones, promptings of the unconscious, suggestions of age-old dreams and fantasies. He has described one such fantasy as the *Dragon Motif* in *The Image in the Rock.* In the following note he alludes to the *Design for a Skyscraper Court:* "As a boy I very rarely saw my mother, and I think that the whole psychological story of what that means to a child is implied in this piece, which is a consistent architectonic statement as well."

He was a searching observer of nature. Endowed with a tenacious visual memory, he would require but a glance or two at an object to add its structure to his wide knowledge of human and animal forms. He never worked directly from a model. If he ever made use of one, it was for purposes of study. On such occasions he would pose the

12

model for a minute or two, walking around and observing intently, and then say, that is enough. He grasped, intuitively perhaps, and managed to suggest in his work the essential nature, the significant gesture of an animal, the cattiness of a cat, the dogginess of a dog, the womanliness of a woman. His drawings have this same rightness and precision of simplification. But, apropos of drawing, he once wrote: "Preparatory drawing seems much like doing one's thinking on paper and then carving the conclusion. I prefer to think the thing out first and last in stone or the medium for which it was intended."

Flannagan had an innate feeling for style. It was apparent in his talk and in his writing, which often had an epigrammatic quality. But it was most evident in his art. He sensed the scope and limitations of his medium and worked within them, using a different approach when carving wood or stone, or modeling clay, or working metal. The great bulk of his work was direct stone carving, but he worked in wood at the beginning and in metal toward the end of his career. His approach to metal working was consistent with his feeling for other materials. "I have used a smooth finish [in the *Rag Doll*] in order to emphasize the form, and because it is truer to the character of the metal. Bronzes lately seem a little inclined to a tricky clay texture. An obvious contradiction. . . ." He was also interested in combining metal and stone.

There was no dross of imitation or second-hand feeling in Flannagan's work. He often spoke of "a realism of feeling rather than a painting or carving of realism." In this sense his sculpture was pure and unalloyed. He was one of the most original of modern sculptors, revealing little outside influence. Each one of his pieces was conceived from within, and grew into an organic and self-contained whole. He never worked with an eye to fashion or the main chance. For every ten artists who function only because conditions are favorable, there is one who cannot help being an artist under any conditions, no matter in what age or country he was born. Flannagan was one of those rare artists.

CARL ZIGROSSER

CHRONOLOGY

1895   Born at Fargo, North Dakota, April 7.

1914–17   Studied painting with Robert Koehler at the Minneapolis Institute of Arts.

1917–22   Shipped as an able-bodied seaman with the Merchant Marine, making several trips to Europe and South America.

1922–23   Worked as a farm hand for Arthur B. Davies at Congers, N. Y. Painted at night, using wax technique Davies taught him. With Davies' encouragement, started to carve in wood.

1923   Exhibited for first time, Montross Gallery, New York, Jan. 23–Feb. 10; 5 "wooden pictures" and 2 wax paintings in 7-man exhibition with Davies, Glackens, Kuhn, the Prendergasts, Sheeler.

1924–29   Lived in New York, Rockland County and Woodstock, N. Y., developing sculpture as his ultimate medium. About 1926, began to work in stone as well as wood; after 1928, gave up wood. In extreme poverty, unable to buy stone, began to use field stone (various glacial boulders). Destroyed paintings and devoted himself to sculpture.

1925   Exhibited, Whitney Studio Club, New York, Dec. 8–24; 21 sculptures in 4-man exhibition with Leon Hartl, Charles Howard, Dorothea Schwarcz.

1927   One-man exhibition, Weyhe Gallery, New York, Jan. 5–20; 26 sculptures.

1928   One-man exhibition, Weyhe Gallery, Jan. 23–Feb. 4.

1929   One-man exhibition, Whitney Studio Galleries, New York, Jan. 22–Feb. 9; 15 sculptures. Contract with Weyhe Gallery guaranteeing weekly stipend in return for sculpture. This arrangement lasted intermittently until 1937.

1930   One-man exhibition, Weyhe Gallery, Apr. 7–26. In May, to Ireland where he lived for a year. Brief visit to Paris.

1931   Returned from Ireland in June. One-man exhibition, Weyhe Gallery, Nov. 9–28; 17 sculptures.

1932–33   Granted Guggenheim Fellowship and returned to Ireland. Lived there from March 1932 to March 1933.

1934   One-man exhibition, Weyhe Gallery. One-man exhibition, Arts Club of Chicago, Mar. 16–30; 26 sculptures. Breakdown, followed by 7 months in New York Hospital at White Plains. There, experimented with metal casting and produced *Toward the Sun* (no. 23) and the *Rag Doll.*

1934–35   First monumental sculpture, *Design for a Skyscraper Court* (see page 27).

1936   One-man exhibition, Weyhe Gallery, Feb. 24–Mar. 14; 24 sculptures. One-man exhibition, Vassar College Art Gallery, Poughkeepsie, N. Y., April; 9 sculptures. Exhibited, Brooklyn Museum, New York, Oct.–Nov.; 10 sculptures in 6-man exhibition with Brook, DuBois, Kroll, Sheeler, Sloan. Commission from Fairmount Park Art Association for monument, the *Gold Miner*, as part of Ellen Phillips Samuel Memorial, Philadelphia. This sculpture, in limestone, 6 feet high, was completed in 1938.

1937   One-man exhibition, Bard College, Annandale-on-Hudson, N. Y., Oct. 27–Nov. 10; 10 sculptures.

1938   One-man exhibition, Weyhe Gallery, Feb. 9–Mar. 5; 27 sculptures.

1939   Survived 4 brain operations. Warned against the effort of cutting stone, he turned to metal, working directly on unfinished bronze casts.

1940   Awarded Alexander Shilling prize allocating *Figure of Dignity* to the Metropolitan Museum of Art, New York.

1942   Died a suicide, January 6. One-man exhibition, Buchholz Gallery, New York. Mar. 18–Apr. 11. 24 sculptures.

Christ. 1925. Walnut, 34″ high. Lent by Frederick
Zimmermann.

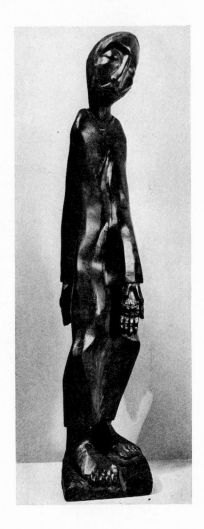

Crouching Woman. 1930. Alabaster,
11 ⅛″ high. Lent by E. Weyhe.

Elephant. 1929–30. Bluestone, 13½″ high. Lent by the Whitney Museum of American Art.

Ram. Ireland, 1931. Granite, 13½″ high. Lent by Edward M. M. Warburg.

Goat. Ireland, 1930–31. Granite, 18½″ long. Lent by the Weyhe Gallery.

Head. Ireland, 1932–33. Granite, 10½″ high. Lent by Mrs. Grace Flannagan.

Sleeping Cat. Ireland, 1932–33. Granite, 21½″ diameter. Lent by Mrs. Malcolm L. McBride.

Dragon Motif. Ireland, 1932–33. Granite, 26″ diameter. Lent by the Weyhe Gallery. (See page 8.)

Note for Dragon Alligator. Brush and ink, 9½ x 8½″. Lent by Curt Valentin.

Evening. Ireland, 1932–33. Black marble, 17″ high. Lent by the Detroit Institute of Arts.

Monkey and Young. Ireland, 1932–33. Granite, 15″ high. Lent by the Addison
Gallery of American Art, Phillips Academy.

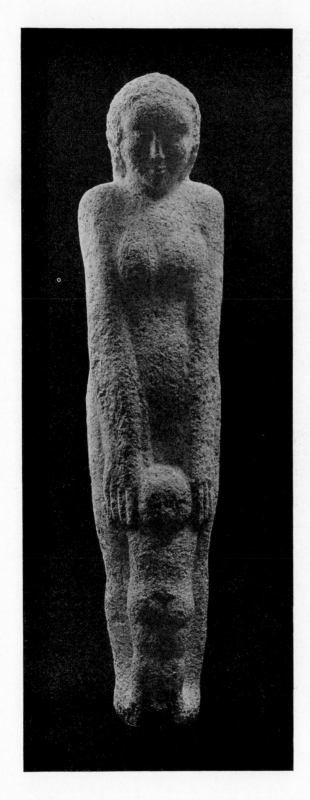

Woman and Child. Ireland, 1932–33.
Granite, 41″ high. Lent by the Vassar
College Art Gallery.

Dragon. Ireland, 1932–33. Granite, 29″ high. Lent by the Weyhe Gallery.

Figure of Dignity. Ireland and
New York, 1932–33. Granite with
cast aluminum horns, 48⅛″ high.
Lent by the Metropolitan Museum
of Art.

Design for a Skyscraper Court: Mother and Child. 1934–35. Red sandstone, 42¾″ high. Lent by the Fogg Museum of Art, Harvard University.

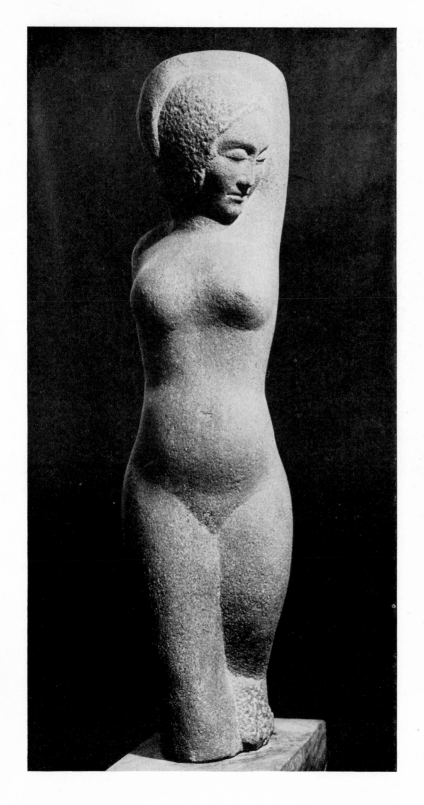

Young Woman (Ron-
do). 1935. Red sand-
stone, 36¾″ high. Lent
by Chauncey Stillman.

Head of a Child. 1935. Quartz, 6½″ high. Lent by the Weyhe Gallery.

Nude. 1941. Brush and ink, 18½″ x 12″. Lent by the Buchholz Gallery.

Nude. 1941. Watercolor, 18 x 11 ⅛″. Lent by John Asmussen.

New One. 1935. Bluestone, 125⁄8″ long. Lent by the Weyhe Gallery.

Restive Acrobat. 1938. Fieldstone, 8″ high.
Lent by Mr. and Mrs. Henry Clifford.

Frog. 1938. Sandstone, 7⅛″
high. Lent by the Wehye Gallery.

32

Snake. 1938. Limestone, 25½″ high. Lent by R. Sturgis Ingersoll.

Little Creature. 1941. Bluestone, 13″ high. Lent by Edgar J. Kaufmann.

Pelican. 1941. Wrought bronze, 17½″ high. Lent by the Buchholz Gallery.

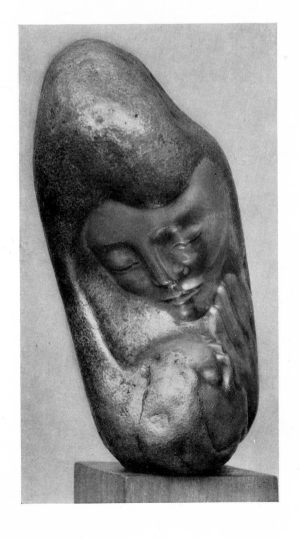

Not Yet. 1940. Wrought bronze, 18″ high. Lent by the Buchholz Gallery.

Dragon Motif. 1941. Bluestone, 12½″ long. Lent by the Buchholz Gallery.

New Lizard—Egg. Brush and ink,
9½ x 9″. Lent by Curt Valentin.